LET'S ROCK

SEDIMENTARY ROCKS

CHRIS OXLADE

Heinemann
LIBRARY

Chicago, Illinois

www.heinemannraintree.com
Visit our website to find out more information about Heinemann-Raintree books.

To order:
☎ Phone 888-454-2279
💻 Visit www.heinemannraintree.com to browse our catalog and order online.

Edited by Louise Galpine and Diyan Leake
Designed by Victoria Allen
Illustrated by Geoff Ward and KJA artists
Picture research by Hannah Taylor
Originated by Capstone Global Library Ltd
Printed and bound in the United States of America, North Mankato, MN

14 13 12
10 9 8 7 6 5 4 3 2

Library of Congress Cataloging-in-Publication Data
Oxlade, Chris.
   Sedimentary rocks / Chris Oxlade.
      p. cm. — (Let's rock)
   Includes bibliographical references and index.
   ISBN 978-1-4329-4681-4 (hb)
   ISBN 978-1-4329-4689-0 (pb)
   1. Rocks, Sedimentary—Juvenile literature. 2. Petrology—Juvenile literature. I. Title.
   QE471.O95 2011
   552'.5—dc22   2010022214

072012
006776RP

Acknowledgments
The author and publisher are grateful to the following for permission to reproduce copyright material: Alamy Images pp. **4** (© Mira), **10** (© Kevin Allen), **11** (© NASA/Landsat/Phil Degginger), **14** (© All Canada Photos), **21** (© Niels Poulsen mus); © Capstone Publishers p. **29** (Karon Dubke); Corbis p. **7** (Frans Lanting); istockphoto p. **18** (© Peter Mukherjee); Photolibrary pp. **9** (Britain on View/Fran Halsall); **12** (imagebroker rf/Gerhard Zwerger-Schoner), **13** (Markus Keller), **20** (Emilio Ereza), **25** (Britain on View/David Noton), **26** (Peter Arnold Images/Ray Pfortner), Science Photo Library pp. **5** (Eye of Science), **8** (David Parker), **16** (Andrew Lambert Photography), **17** (Dirk Wiersma).

Cover photograph of Grand Canyon National Park, Arizona, reproduced with permission of Photolibrary (Dan Leffel).

We would like to thank Dr. Stuart Robinson for his invaluable help in the preparation of this book.

Every effort has been made to contact copyright holders of any material reproduced in this book. Any omissions will be rectified in subsequent printings if notice is given to the publisher.

Disclaimer
All the Internet addresses (URLs) given in this book were valid at the time of going to press. However, due to the dynamic nature of the Internet, some addresses may have changed, or sites may have changed or ceased to exist since publication. While the author and publisher regret any inconvenience this may cause readers, no responsibility for any such changes can be accepted by either the author or the publisher.

CONTENTS

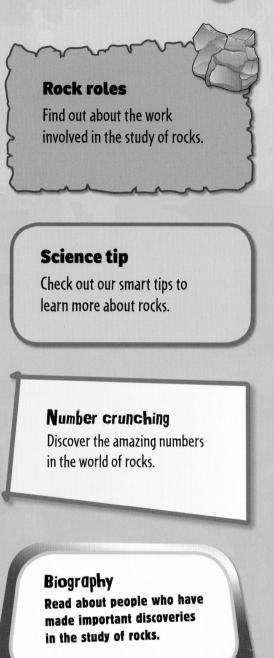

Rock roles
Find out about the work involved in the study of rocks.

Science tip
Check out our smart tips to learn more about rocks.

Number crunching
Discover the amazing numbers in the world of rocks.

Biography
Read about people who have made important discoveries in the study of rocks.

Some words are printed in bold, **like this**. You can find out what they mean by looking in the glossary on page 30.

WHAT ARE SEDIMENTARY ROCKS?

Imagine a river, colored brown with mud, flowing into the sea. The mud settles on the seabed. It is slowly buried as more mud comes down the river. Over millions of years the water is squeezed out and great **pressure** turns the mud into new rock. The mud is called **sediment**, and the new rock is called sedimentary rock. Sedimentary rocks are one of the types of rock that make up Earth.

MINERALS AND CRYSTALS

All rocks, not just sedimentary rocks, are made from materials called **minerals**. Some rocks are made from just one mineral, but most are made from a mixture of different minerals.

Minerals themselves are made up of **atoms**. In all minerals, these are arranged neatly in rows and columns. Materials with their atoms arranged like this are called **crystals**.

In the Badlands National Park, in South Dakota, you can see different colored layers of sedimentary rocks.

New sedimentary rocks are constantly being made, and old sedimentary rocks are being destroyed all the time. This is part of a process called the **rock cycle**. In this book we follow the journey of sedimentary rock as it moves around the rock cycle.

Rock role

Sedimentary rock is just one type of rock. The other two types are **igneous rock** and **metamorphic rock**. Igneous rock is made when **molten** rock cools and becomes solid. Metamorphic rock is formed when rocks are changed by heat and pressure.

These are crystals of **quartz**, which is a very common mineral in sedimentary rocks. Quartz is usually transparent. These crystals have been colored to show up in the photograph.

WHAT IS INSIDE EARTH?

You can see bare rock at coasts, in mountains, and where roads are cut into hills. This rock is part of a layer of solid rock called Earth's **crust**. The crust is the surface layer of Earth. It is between 25 and 90 kilometers (15 and 56 miles) thick, and it sits on top of very hot rock below. This hot rock forms a layer 2,900 kilometers (1,800 miles) deep called the **mantle**. Beneath the mantle is Earth's **core**, where the temperature reaches 5,500 degrees Celsius (9,932 degrees Fahrenheit).

A cutaway diagram shows the main layers inside Earth. The crust is very thin compared to the other layers.

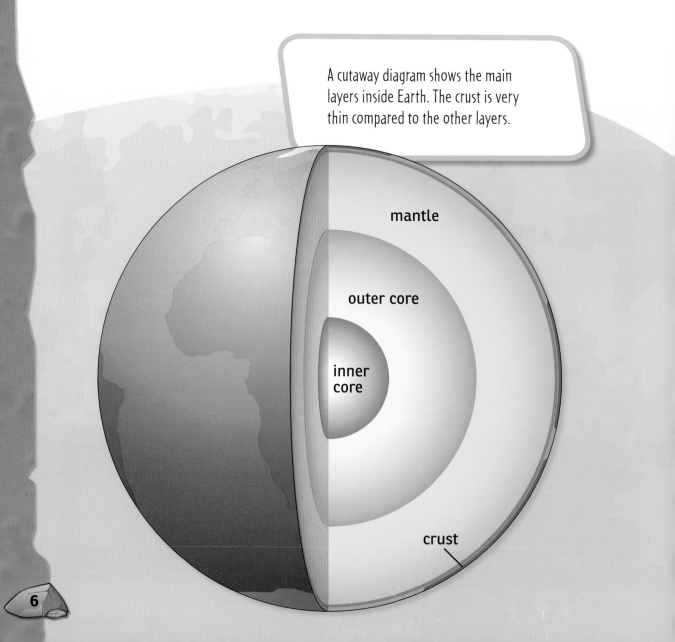

mantle

outer core

inner core

crust

THE ROCK CYCLE

During the **rock cycle**, rocks are constantly changing. New rocks, including sedimentary rocks, are always being made. The rocks move through the crust and may be destroyed or **recycled** into other sorts of rocks. These changes take place very slowly. It can take millions of years for a sedimentary rock to be formed, to make its journey through the crust, and then to be destroyed—either on the surface or deep inside the crust.

Number crunching

The crust is a mixture of the three different types of rock. About 95 percent of the crust is **igneous rock**. Most of this igneous rock is under the oceans. Only a small percentage of the crust is made up of **metamorphic rock**.

New igneous rocks are made at the surface when lava from **volcanoes** cools and becomes solid. This lava flow is on the island of Hawaii.

WHERE DOES SEDIMENT COME FROM?

Some sedimentary rocks are made from millions of tiny **particles** of rock. The journey of sedimentary rock starts where these particles are made. Other sedimentary rocks are made from the countless skeletons or shells of sea creatures (see page 14).

BREAKING UP OLD ROCKS

Rocks on Earth's surface are worn away by natural processes called **weathering** and **erosion**. Weathering is the way the climate breaks up rock. For example, in cold places, water that trickles into cracks in rocks expands when it freezes, widening the cracks. In deserts, extreme heat in the day and extreme cold at night makes rocks grow and shrink, which weakens them. Erosion takes place when flowing water, wind, and **glaciers** break rock up and carry particles away as **sediment**.

These strange **sandstone** pillars are being weathered by changing temperatures and by sand blown around their bases.

WHAT IS SEDIMENT?

Sediment is the name for the particles of rock that are carried by flowing water, glaciers, and the wind. In a river, very tiny particles are carried in the water, and larger particles bump along the riverbed.

Science tip

The next time you cross a river bridge or walk by a river, look for sediments in the river. If the water looks brown, it is carrying lots of sediment. You might see pebbles or larger rocks that have been carried downstream. You might also see sediments left on the riverbanks.

You can often see cliffs of weathered **limestone** along a coast.

HOW ARE SEDIMENTARY ROCKS MADE?

The **sediment** carried in rivers or **glaciers**, or blown by the wind, eventually comes to a stop. It builds up to form layers, which are also called sediments. Sediments are normally washed away or blown away again, but sometimes more sediment buries them. That is the next stage in the journey—when sedimentary rocks start to be made.

LAYING DOWN SEDIMENTS

When the water in a river that is carrying **particles** along slows down, the particles settle to the bottom of the water and form layers of sediment. Sediments form on riverbeds and on the seabed at the mouths of large rivers. Sediments also form on beaches and in sandbanks. In deserts, sediments blown by the wind build up into sand dunes.

Sandbanks in Great Britain's Severn Estuary formed from sediment washed down the river.

SOFT SEDIMENTS TO SOLID ROCK

When sediments are buried deep under more sediments, water is squeezed out and the particles get more tightly packed together. At the same time, chemicals in the water form **crystals** between the particles, sticking them together like glue. The result is new sedimentary rock.

Sediments are often left on the seabed at the mouths of rivers, forming new land called deltas. This is the Mississippi Delta, in Mississippi.

Rock roles

A **geologist** is a scientist who studies how rocks are made, how they change, and how they make up Earth. Some jobs that geologists do are related to sedimentary rocks. For example, some geologists study sediments, some study **fossils**, and some look for oil and gas in rocks (see pages 14-15).

LAYERS IN SEDIMENTARY ROCKS

You can often see different layers of sediments in cliffs made from sedimentary rocks. The different layers are made when particles of different shapes or sizes are left on top of each other. For example, a layer of larger particles might be laid on top of a layer of smaller particles. Newer sedimentary rocks are always formed on top of older rocks.

At the Grand Canyon, in Arizona, layers of sedimentary rocks called **sandstone** and **limestone** that are more than 2 kilometers (nearly a mile and a half) deep can be seen.

The sedimentary rocks of the Grand Canyon formed between 550 and 250 million years ago.

ROCKS FROM ANIMALS AND PLANTS

Some sedimentary rocks are not made from particles of older rocks. They are formed from the skeletons and shells of sea creatures, and sometimes from the remains of plants. When the animals die, their shells and skeletons sink to the bottom of the sea. Over millions of years, deep sediments build up, and the buried sediments turn into rock.

Other sedimentary rocks are made when water that contains **minerals evaporates** (dries up). These rocks are therefore called evaporites. The evaporation allows crystals of minerals to grow. This is how rock salt is formed.

Science tip

A coastal area is a good place to look for layers of sedimentary rocks. Many cliffs are made of sedimentary rocks, and you can often see layers of different colors or sizes of particles in them. The sand and pebbles on a beach may be made from **eroded** rocks in the cliff above.

The White Cliffs of Dover, in England, are made from chalk, which is formed from millions of microscopic skeletons.

13

FOSSILS IN SEDIMENTARY ROCKS

Fossils are the remains of plants and animals that lived thousands or millions of years ago. Fossils are formed when animals or plants that die are buried in layers of sediments that gradually become rock. Fossils are an important source of information about plants and animals that lived in the past.

Plant fossils are made when plant material is buried. With animals, the skeleton or shell is left in the rock and is replaced with new minerals as the rock forms, or otherwise a hole is left in the rock. Some types of limestone (a sedimentary rock) are made completely of the shells and skeletons of sea animals.

These archaeologists are digging out the fossilized skeleton of a dinosaur in Canada. The dinosaur was buried in sediment tens of thousands of years ago.

WHAT ARE FOSSIL FUELS?

Coal, oil, and gas are called fossil fuels. They are made from the remains of plants and animals that were buried in sediments millions of years ago. Coal is made from fossilized plant remains. Oil and gas come from the remains of **plankton** (plant-like living things) and algae that were changed by heat and **pressure** deep underground. They are trapped in the tiny spaces between the particles of sedimentary rocks.

Rock roles

Geophysics is the science of detecting the structure of rocks deep underground. Geophysicists use special equipment for the job, such as machines that send waves of sound into Earth and detect waves that bounce back off different rocks. Many geophysicists work in the oil industry, looking for rocks that might be full of oil and gas.

Oil and gas are found trapped in layers of sedimentary rock. Drilling into the rock releases the oil and gas.

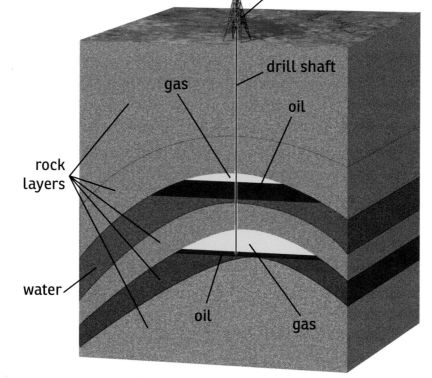

oil well

drill shaft

gas

oil

rock layers

water

oil

gas

WHAT TYPES OF SEDIMENTARY ROCK ARE THERE?

Here are some examples of sedimentary rocks:

Sandstone is made from **grains** of sand stuck together. It has a rough texture, like sandpaper. The grains are rounded and made mainly of the **mineral quartz**.

Gritstone is similar to sandstone, but its **particles** are larger and not rounded, so it feels rougher.

Mudstone is made of small particles of rock that are too small to see without a microscope. It is black, gray, red, or green and is very brittle.

Clay has extremely small particles, which are too small to see even with a microscope. Clay becomes soft and easy to break when it is wet.

Conglomerate is made of a mixture of different sizes of rounded rocks, such as pebbles, boulders, and sand.

Limestones are mostly made from shells and **fossils**. For example, shelly limestone is full of small shells. Chalk is a type of limestone made from tiny pieces of calcite (a mineral). The calcite is made by **plankton** and falls to the bottom of the sea when the plankton die.

This is a sample of sandstone, which is a sedimentary rock. You can see the rough texture of the rock.

Identifying sedimentary rocks

Sedimentary rocks are normally dull rather than shiny, and they do not have **crystals**. It is often easy to break grains off them. Any rock with fossils is normally a sedimentary rock, too. Use the table here to help you identify which sedimentary rock is which.

Rock	Grain	Color	Hardness
sandstone	medium	red/brown	hard
mudstone	fine	black/gray/red/green	hard
clay	fine	red/brown	soft
conglomerate	mixed	red/brown	medium
shelly limestone	medium with shells	brown/gray	medium
chalk	fine	white	soft

This odd-looking rock is a type of limestone called coquina. It is made mostly of the shells of sea animals, including snails.

STALACTITES AND STALAGMITES

If you have ever visited a cave, you might have seen rocky spikes. They are made from a type of limestone, a sedimentary rock. The limestone is **dissolved** in water that drips from the cave roof. As the water evaporates, the limestone is left behind and grows into **stalactites**, which hang down from the roof, and **stalagmites**, which form upward from the floor. Travertine is similar. It grows around hot springs, where hot water comes out of the ground.

HOW DO WE KNOW HOW OLD SEDIMENTARY ROCKS ARE?

Geologists often need to find out how old rocks are. For example, the age of a piece of shelly limestone is a clue for a geologist trying to reconstruct the journey that limestone has taken.

Fossils in a sedimentary rock can show the age of the rock. This is because different animals have lived on Earth at different times in the past, and geologists have a record of which fossils come from which time.

Limestone stalactites like these take thousands of years to form as water drips down from the cave roof.

Another way of dating some sedimentary rocks is called radiometric dating. This process relies on the fact that, over time, some types of **atom** change into other types. (This process is called radioactive decay.) The amount of various types of atom in a sample is measured to figure out the age.

Geologists also know that where one layer of sedimentary rock lies on top of another, the uppermost rock is younger. This is because its sediment must have been laid on top of older, existing rock.

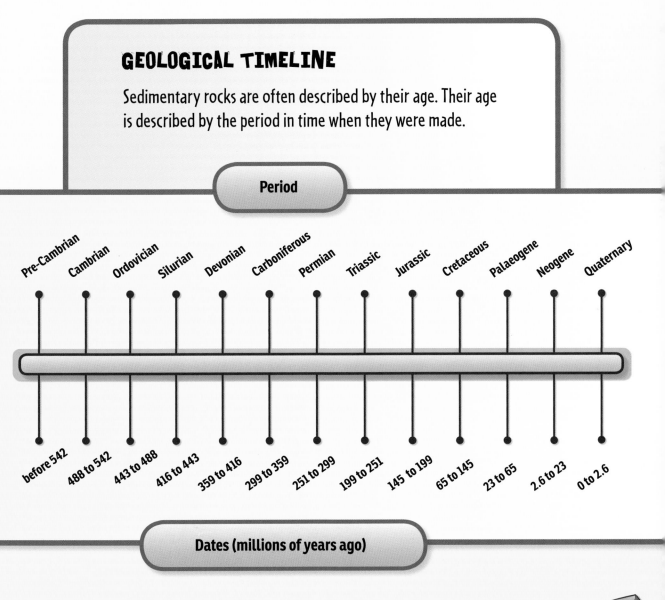

GEOLOGICAL TIMELINE

Sedimentary rocks are often described by their age. Their age is described by the period in time when they were made.

Period

Period	Dates (millions of years ago)
Pre-Cambrian	before 542
Cambrian	488 to 542
Ordovician	443 to 488
Silurian	416 to 443
Devonian	359 to 416
Carboniferous	299 to 359
Permian	251 to 299
Triassic	199 to 251
Jurassic	145 to 199
Cretaceous	65 to 145
Palaeogene	23 to 65
Neogene	2.6 to 23
Quaternary	0 to 2.6

WHAT DO WE USE SEDIMENTARY ROCKS FOR?

Sedimentary rocks are useful materials. Builders make walls, roof tiles, and paving slabs from **sandstone**, gritstone, and **limestone**. Gardeners also decorate gardens with them. These rocks are strong, although some sorts of sandstone and limestone are not suitable for building because they are easily affected by **weathering**.

Crushed limestone is used to make concrete and for road surfaces. When crushed limestone is heated up, it turns into a material called lime. Lime is an ingredient in cement, which in turn is used to make concrete.

This potter is shaping clay into a pot. Clay is a soft sedimentary rock made from very tiny **particles** of rock.

SEDIMENTARY ROCKS IN THE PAST

Tens of thousands of years ago, people made simple tools from flint. Lumps of flint are found in chalk. Flint is easy to chip into shapes, and the chips often have sharp edges. So, flint was used to make simple knives, axes, and arrow heads for hunting and preparing meat.

Clay has been used for more than 10,000 years to make pots and building bricks. The pyramids of ancient Egypt were covered in limestone.

These flint daggers were made thousands of years ago. You can see where the flint was chipped away.

Rock roles

A stonemason is a person who cuts and carves rock into parts for buildings and sculptures. Stonemasons need plenty of skill and patience to carve rock accurately without making mistakes. Modern stonemasons often prepare new pieces of stone to repair very old buildings, including the great cathedrals of Europe, such as Nôtre Dame in Paris.

DO SEDIMENTARY ROCKS LAST FOREVER?

Now we have arrived at the final stage in the journey of sedimentary rocks. Sedimentary rocks can last a very, very long time. For example, a **limestone** that is being **eroded** on a mountaintop today might have been made at the bottom of an ocean 100 million years ago. But whatever happens to sedimentary rocks, they do not last forever. Eventually they are destroyed or changed into other rocks.

WHERE SEDIMENTARY ROCKS ARE DESTROYED

Earth's **crust** is cracked into many giant pieces called **tectonic plates**. In some places where the plates meet, one plate slides under another. The plate sinks down into the **mantle**. Any sedimentary rocks in the plate are destroyed. Over a period of time, the **minerals** in the plate may become **igneous rock** again inside **volcanoes**.

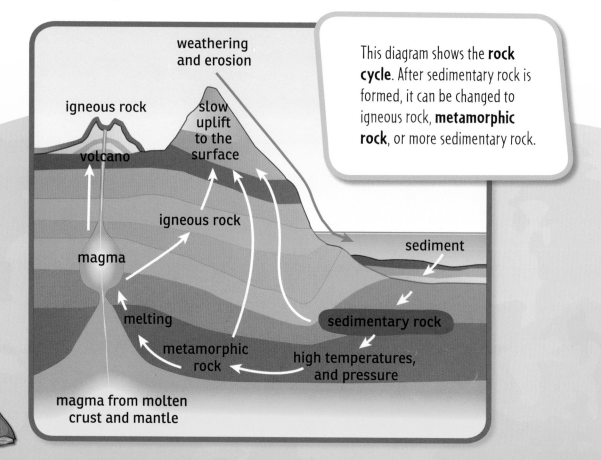

weathering and erosion

igneous rock

slow uplift to the surface

volcano

igneous rock

magma

melting

metamorphic rock

sediment

sedimentary rock

high temperatures, and pressure

magma from molten crust and mantle

This diagram shows the **rock cycle**. After sedimentary rock is formed, it can be changed to igneous rock, **metamorphic rock**, or more sedimentary rock.

Other sedimentary rocks may be pushed upward in the crust. When rocks above them are worn away, the sedimentary rocks reach the surface. Then they are eroded, too. The **particles** of rock may go on to make new sedimentary rocks.

Here two tectonic plates are moving toward each other. Sedimentary rocks on the seafloor are crumpled and destroyed by the movement of the plates.

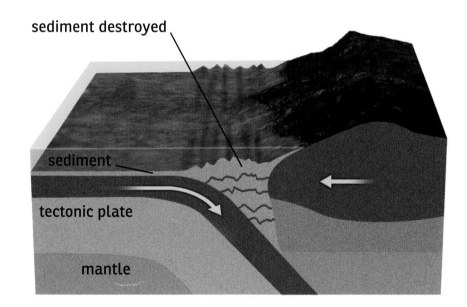

sediment destroyed

sediment

tectonic plate

mantle

SEDIMENTARY TO METAMORPHIC

Sometimes sedimentary rocks are changed into metamorphic rocks. This happens in two ways. First, sedimentary rocks are changed when they are heated up by **magma** flowing nearby. Second, they are changed when they are compressed deep underground. This normally happens where mountains are pushed up by two tectonic plates crashing into each other. Examples of metamorphic rocks made from sedimentary rocks are slate or a rock called **schist**, which are both formed from shale, and **marble**, which is formed from limestone.

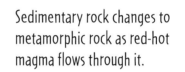

Sedimentary rock changes to metamorphic rock as red-hot magma flows through it.

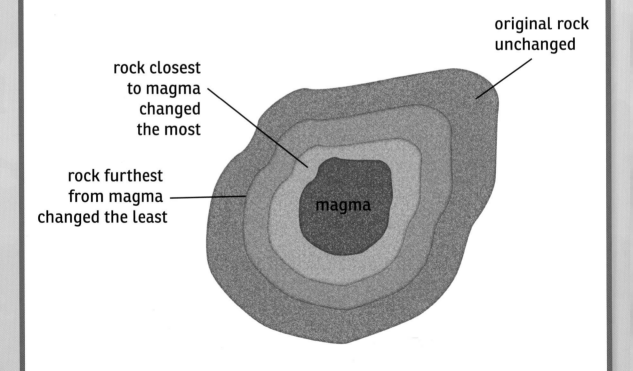

original rock unchanged

rock closest to magma changed the most

rock furthest from magma changed the least

magma

MAKING CAVES

Limestone caves form because rainwater slowly **dissolves** the limestone. The water trickles down through cracks in the rock The rock at the edges of the cracks dissolves and the cracks get wider. Over thousands of years, the cracks become caves and passages through the rock. Limestone caves often contain amazing rock features such as **stalactites** and **stalagmites** (see page 18). The cave roofs sometimes collapse, leaving strange landscapes of limestone towers.

BIOGRAPHY

William Smith (1769–1839) was an English engineer and geologist. While digging the canals in England, Smith noticed that the same layers of sedimentary rock appeared in different places. He realized that these rock layers, perhaps hundreds of miles apart, must have been made at the same time. Smith went on to draw the first geological map of the British Isles.

This flat, rocky area is made of limestone. Deep grooves have been made in it as rainwater dissolves the rock.

ARE WE HARMING SEDIMENTARY ROCKS?

People have been using sedimentary rocks for tens of thousands of years, and sedimentary rocks are still an important resource for us. Where rocks are near the surface, we dig them out in **quarries**, destroying the natural rocks and creating deep holes. Quarries are unsightly, but more importantly, digging out the rocks creates dust and noise **pollution**.

Walkers and climbers in mountains can easily **erode** sedimentary rocks. The rocks can also be harmed by **acid** rain, which is rain made into an acid by pollution in the air.

Quarrying and **erosion** are unlikely ever to stop the movement of sedimentary rocks through the **rock cycle**. Even so, we should try not to damage sedimentary rocks, as they are part of our natural environment.

The detail on these **limestone** statues in New York has been destroyed by acid rain.

JOURNEY'S END

Our journey of sedimentary rocks is complete. The journey began with rocks on the surface of Earth that were eroded into rocky **particles**, or the remains of sea organisms. The particles or remains formed layers of **sediment**. Layer upon layer of sediment was squeezed together and very slowly turned to solid rock.

The journey of sedimentary rock that we have followed is all part of the rock cycle. The cycle has been going on since Earth was formed 4.5 billion years ago, and it will continue for billions of years in the future.

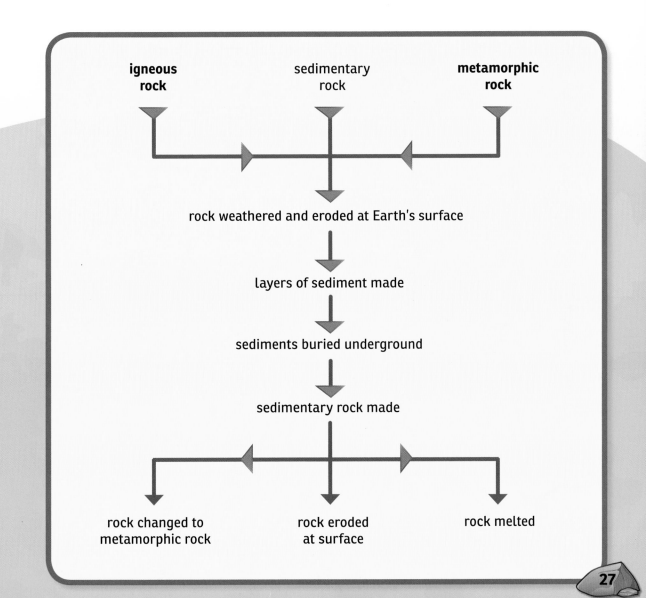

MAKE YOUR OWN SEDIMENT!

Here's a simple project that will help you to understand the journey of sedimentary rocks that we have followed through this book. Before you try the experiment, read the instructions, collect the materials you need, and prepare an area where you can work.

You should ask an adult's permission before you start the experiment.

YOU WILL NEED:

- two old trays
- play sand
- a jug
- water.

WHAT TO DO:

1. Spread a few handfuls of sand over one of the trays and sprinkle water over it to make it damp.

2. Rest one end of the tray on another tray (so that the trays overlap). Lift the other end of the first tray up a few inches.

3. Slowly pour water onto the top of the first tray. What happens to the sand?

The flowing water in the top tray carries away the **particles** of rock in the sand. It carries them into the bottom tray. Here, the water slows down and the particles settle to the bottom of the water and stop. They build up into layers of **sediment**. You can see how flowing water moves particles of rock and creates sediments that form sedimentary rock.

GLOSSARY

acid substance, usually liquid, that can damage things it touches if it is very strong

atom smallest particle of chemical matter that can exist

canal human-made waterway

clay common sedimentary rock that is soft and has very fine grains

core central part of Earth

crust rocky surface layer of Earth

crystal piece of material in which atoms are organized in neat rows and columns

dissolve completely mix with a liquid

erode wear away

erosion wearing away of rocks by flowing water, wind, and glaciers

evaporate process of changing from a liquid to a gas

fossil remains of an ancient animal or plant found in sedimentary rock

geological map map that shows which rocks make up the surface of Earth

geologist scientist who studies the rocks and soil from which Earth is made

glacier slow-moving river of ice that flows down from a mountain range

grain particles in a rock (the particles can be crystals or small pieces of rock)

igneous rock rock formed when magma (molten rock) cools and solidifies

limestone common sedimentary rock made up of the mineral calcite, which can come from the shells and skeletons of sea animals

magma molten rock below Earth's crust

mantle very deep layer of hot rock below Earth's crust

marble metamorphic rock made from the sedimentary rock limestone

metamorphic rock rock formed when rocks are changed by heat and pressure

mineral substance that is naturally present in Earth, such as gold and salt

molten hot liquid

particle small piece of material

plankton microscopic sea animals and plants

pollution harmful substances that are released into the air, water, or soil.

pressure force or weight pressing against something

quarry place where large amounts of rock are dug out of the ground

quartz hard mineral, often found in crystal form

recycle process of changing something into something new

rock cycle constant formation, destruction, and recycling of rocks through Earth's crust

sandstone common sedimentary rock made from grains of sand stuck together

schist common medium-grained metamorphic rock

sediment rocky particles made either by weathering and erosion or by the remains of sea animals or plants

stalactite long, rocky spike hanging down from the roof of a cave

stalagmite long, rocky spike growing up from the floor of a cave

tectonic plate one of the giant pieces that Earth's crust is cracked into

volcano opening in Earth's surface where magma escapes from underground

weathering breaking up of rocks by weather conditions such as extremes of temperature

FIND OUT MORE

BOOKS

Faulkner, Rebecca. *Sedimentary Rock* (Geology Rocks!). Chicago: Raintree, 2008.

Pipe, Jim. *Earth's Rocks and Fossils* (Planet Earth). Pleasantville, N.Y.: Gareth Stevens, 2008.

Walker, Sally M. *Rocks* (Early Bird Earth Science). Minneapolis: Lerner, 2007.

WEBSITES

See animations of how rocks are formed at this website of the Franklin Institute: **www.fi.edu/fellows/fellow1/oct98/create**

Find lots of information about rocks and minerals, as well as links to other interesting websites, at this site: **www.rocksforkids.com**

PLACES TO VISIT

American Museum of Natural History
Central Park West at 79th Street
New York, New York, 10024-5192
Tel: (212) 769-5100
www.amnh.org
Visit a large and fascinating collection of rocks, minerals, and fossils.

The Field Museum
1400 S. Lake Shore Drive
Chicago, Illinois 60605-2496
Tel: (312) 922-9410
www.fieldmuseum.org
See fascinating exhibits of rocks, minerals, and fossils from around the world.

INDEX